THIS BOOK BELONGS TO

David

Einsidler

The Old Testament

MOST OF THE EVENTS OF THE Old
Testament take place in a small area to the east of
the Mediterranean Sea. From ancient times
people have lived and traveled along a strip of
land known as the "fertile crescent", which
stretches from Egypt, through Canaan and
Mesopotamia to Babylonia.
There was enough water in this
area to enable them to grow
crops and graze animals.
Canaan, the "promised land",
where the Israelites flourished, is
only about 150 miles (230km)
from north to south. It contains
many different types of scenery,
including plains and river
valleys suitable for farming,
lakes, hills, and rocky desert.

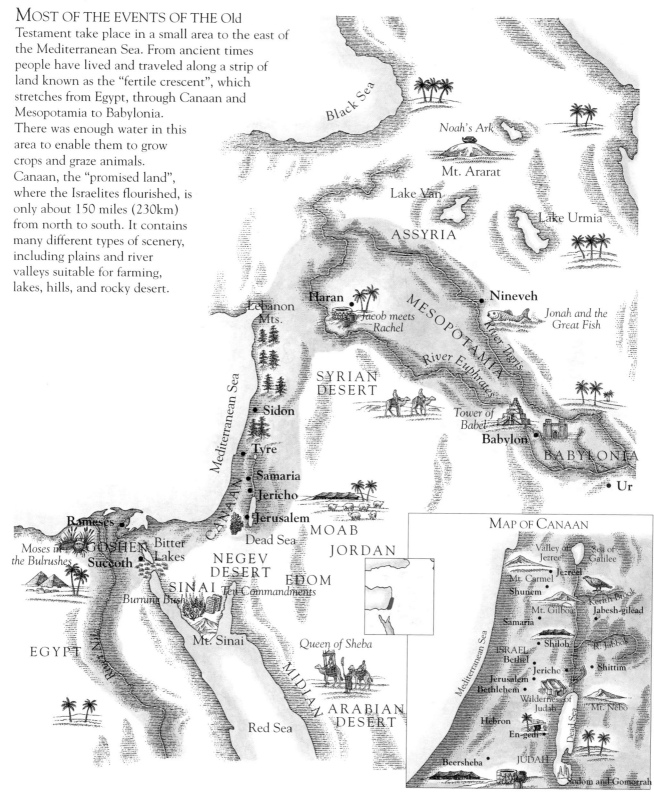

Black Sea

Noah's Ark

Mt. Ararat

Lake Van

Lake Urmia

ASSYRIA

Nineveh

Jonah and the
Great Fish

Lebanon
Mts.

Haran

Jacob meets
Rachel

MESOPOTAMIA

River Tigris

River Euphrates

SYRIAN
DESERT

Sidon

Tower of
Babel

Babylon

BABYLONIA

Tyre

Mediterranean Sea

Samaria

Jericho

Jerusalem

Ur

Dead Sea

MOAB

JORDAN

Rameses

Moses in
the Bulrushes

GOSHEN

Bitter
Lakes

NEGEV
DESERT

EDOM

MAP OF CANAAN

Succoth

SINAI

Ten Commandments

Valley of
Jezreel

Sea of
Galilee

Burning Bush

Mt. Carmel

Jezreel

EGYPT

Mt. Sinai

Queen of Sheba

Shunem

Mt. Gilboa

Kerith Brook

Jabesh-gilead

Samaria

Shiloh

ISRAEL

R. Jabbok

Bethel

Jericho

Shittim

MIDIAN

Jerusalem

Bethlehem

Wilderness of
Judah

Mt. Nebo

ARABIAN
DESERT

Hebron

Mediterranean Sea

Dead Sea

Red Sea

En-gedi

Beersheba

JUDAH

Sodom and Gomorrah

David & Goliath

• And other Bible stories •
—— Retold *by* Selina Hastings ——

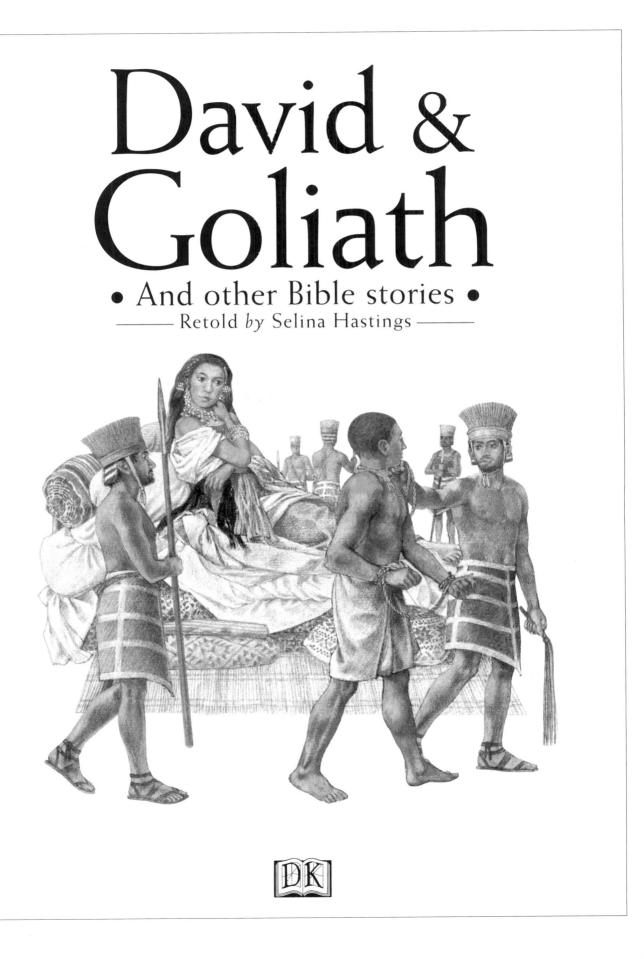

DK

A DK PUBLISHING BOOK

Art Editor Shirley Gwillym
Project Editor Marie Greenwood
Senior Editor Emma Johnson
Designer Sarah Cowley
Additional design by Heather Blackham, Muffy Dodson
Production Ruth Cobb, Marguerite Fenn
Managing Editor Susan Peach
Managing Art Editor Jacquie Gulliver

Introduction and section openers written by
Geoffrey Marshall-Taylor

CONSULTANTS
Educational Consultant
Geoffrey Marshall-Taylor,
Executive Producer, BBC Education,
Responsible for religious radio programmes
for schools

Historical Consultant
Jonathan Tubb,
Western Asiatic Department
British Museum, London

Religious Consultants
Mary Evans
London Bible College

Jenny Nemko
Jewish writer and broadcaster
for the BBC

Published in the United States by
DK PUBLISHING, Inc.,
95 Madison Avenue, New York, NY 10016

The Children's Illustrated Bible
Copyright © 1994 Dorling Kindersley Limited, London
Text copyright © 1994 Selina Hastings
The right of Selina Hastings to be identified as the Author
of this Work has been asserted by her in accordance with
the Copyright Designs and Patents Act 1988.

A CIP catalog record for this book is available from the
Library of Congress.

ISBN 07513-5484-8
Reproduced by Colourscan, Singapore
Printed and bound in Spain by Artes Graficas
Toledo S.A.   DL:TO-327-1996

Extracts from the Authorised Version of the Bible (The
King James Bible), the rights of which are vested in the
Crown, are reproduced by permission of the Crown's
Patentee, Cambridge University Press.

CONTENTS

Introduction to the Bible

MEDIEVAL BIBLE
A decorative page from an 8th-century Bible in the Royal Library in Stockholm.

THE BIBLE IS A collection of books written by different people during more than 1,000 years and dating from about 1450 BC. It is divided into two main parts, the Old Testament (or Hebrew Testament) and the New Testament.

The Old Testament books are the Scriptures, or sacred writings, of the Jewish people. They give an account of the people of ancient Israel over many centuries. By contrast, the New Testament, which consists of writings about Jesus and his first followers, covers a period of about 60 or 70 years. Both the Old and New Testaments make up the Christian Bible.

There are 66 books in the Bible. It is often said that it is more like a library because there are so many kinds of writing in it. For example, there are books containing laws, history, poetry, wise sayings or proverbs, diaries, and letters.

The Old Testament

The 39 books of the Old Testament have guided the Jewish people throughout their history. These are the Scriptures which Jesus read. For Jews, the most important part is the Torah – the first five books of the Bible. The word "Torah" means "teaching." The five books are Genesis, Exodus, Leviticus, Numbers, and Deuteronomy. Christians call this the "Pentateuch," a Greek word meaning "five books."

Each Sabbath Jewish congregations listen to a part of the Torah being read from scrolls in the synagogue. It takes a year of weekly readings to go from the beginning to the end. On the day when the last part of the Torah is reached and Genesis chapter one is due to be read again, there is a celebration called *Simchat Torah*, the "rejoicing of the law." A procession dances around the synagogue carrying the Torah scrolls high in thanksgiving.

In Christian services passages from the Old Testament are often read. The stories are considered important by Christians because of what can be learned from them about God, about others, and about themselves.

The Five Books of Moses

The Torah is special to Jews because its books contain God's words given through Moses to the Hebrew people, their ancestors. The Torah is sometimes referred to as "The Five Books of Moses" because of this. Its stories, songs, prayers, and laws teach about God and what he promises to his people and expects from them.

On Mount Sinai, Moses received God's laws.

For Christians, all the books of the Old Testament are equally important. They are divided into four sections: the law, history, poetry and wisdom writings, and the prophets.

At first the words of the earliest books of the Old Testament were passed on by one generation repeating them to the next. Eventually they were written down in the Hebrew language on parchment, which is made from animal skin. Each word was copied carefully by a scribe, as it is today.

A rabbi, or teacher, studies the words of the Torah.

A Jewish boy becomes Bar-Mitvah at the age of 13.

The Torah is studied by young Jews from an early age. When a Jewish boy reaches the age of 13 he becomes *Bar-Mitzvah*, which means "a son of the commandment." He is now a Jewish adult and, on the Sabbath after his birthday, he can read from the Torah in the synagogue. A Jewish girl becomes *Bat-Mitzvah* (daughter of the commandment) at the age of 12. In many synagogues she can also read from the Torah.

The Dead Sea Scrolls

In 1947 a shepherd boy came across some ancient scrolls in caves near the Dead Sea: they were fragments of all the books of the Old Testament, except for Esther, and had probably been written about the time of Jesus. It is thought that they came from the monastery at Qumran and were hidden in the caves by a group of Jews called the Essenes. The discovery showed how accurately scribes had copied these special words throughout the centuries.

Psalm 119 verse 105 explains why the Old Testament is so important to Jews and Christians. The writer says to God, "Thy word is a lamp unto my feet and a light unto my path."

DISCOVERY
The Dead Sea Scrolls, stored in pottery jars, were found in caves at Qumran (below). Some of the fragments date back to the 2nd century BC.

The Promised Land

CLUSTER OF GRAPES
The large, juicy grapes brought back from Canaan were important to the Israelites. Grapes could be eaten fresh, dried as raisins, boiled to make grape syrup, or pressed to make wine.

FROM HIS CAMP IN THE PARAN DESERT, Moses sent twelve men to spy out Canaan, the land which God had promised to the people of Israel. The men carefully explored the country, and after forty days returned, bringing with them handfuls of grapes, figs, and pomegranates.

"It is a rich country flowing with milk and honey," they told Moses and Aaron. "But the people are strong and they live in great walled cities. We would never be able to overcome them."

In spite of this report, Caleb, from the tribe of Judah, was eager to invade at once and take possession of the country. But the others,

AND THEY TOLD HIM, "WE CAME UNTO THE LAND WHITHER THOU SENTEST US, AND SURELY IT FLOWETH WITH MILK AND HONEY."
NUMBERS 13:27

The men return from Canaan, bringing with them grapes, figs, and pomegranates

Moses   Joshua

*Moses calls Joshua and says that he must
lead the people into Canaan*

who had been with him on the expedition, were afraid. "We would be defeated," they said. And to make their argument convincing, they pretended they had seen a race of giants in Canaan, beside whom the Israelites would look like grasshoppers.

For forty years the children of Israel continued to wander in the wilderness. In time Aaron died, and Moses knew that he, too, would soon die. He called Joshua, son of Nun, and said, "I am old and will never reach Canaan. You must lead our people there. Be strong and of good heart. Do not be afraid, for God will be with you."

Then Moses inscribed the law of God on two tablets of stone, for he knew that without his guidance the Israelites would soon take to evil ways. The priests kept the tablets in a golden chest called the Ark of the Covenant, which had been made as a holy resting place for the ten commandments.

Having blessed his people, Moses went to the summit of Mount Pisgah where God showed him the whole of the promised land, stretching from Gilead, Dan, Judah, and the distant sea in the west to the southern valley of Jericho, city of palm trees.

There Moses died and was buried, and the people wept for thirty days. Since his death there has never been a prophet like him in Israel. He was a man who had the courage to defy Pharaoh and lead his people out of Egypt; a man who stood face to face with God.

CANAAN
In the northern part of Canaan is the valley of Jezreel (pictured here). Although known as a land "flowing with milk and honey", Canaan is a land of variety. The area descends from fertile hills and fields to a barren desert watered by springs.

The Battle of Jericho

The priests carry the Ark of the Covenant across the River Jordan, which had stopped flowing

AFTER THE TWO MESSENGERS had returned from Jericho, they reported to Joshua, and he assembled all his people on the banks of the Jordan. "Listen carefully to what I have to say. As soon as the priests carrying the Ark of the Covenant put their feet in the water, the river will stop flowing. The waters coming from the source will cease, and a path of dry land will appear. On this you will all be able to cross safely to the other side." And it happened exactly as Joshua had described. The people left their tents and came down to the riverbank; the priests lifted up the Ark and approached the water. At once the waters stopped and divided, and the priests walked to the middle of the riverbed. There they stood, holding the Ark up high, while all of Joshua's people passed safely to the far side. The priests

The Israelite army circles the city

The seven priests blow their trumpets made from rams' horns

"WHEN THEY MAKE A LONG BLAST WITH THE RAM'S HORN, AND WHEN YE HEAR THE SOUND OF THE TRUMPET, ALL THE PEOPLE SHALL SHOUT WITH A GREAT SHOUT; AND THE WALL OF THE CITY SHALL FALL DOWN FLAT."
JOSHUA 6:5

then followed, and no sooner had they stepped onto dry land, than the waters closed over behind them.

Joshua then gathered his army together. Over forty-thousand men stood ready to fight on the plains of Jericho. All of them were willing to die for Joshua, for he was as inspiring a leader as Moses: his people both trusted him and feared his anger, for they knew that, like Moses, he was loved by God.

Jericho was in a state of siege, the gates bolted shut against the Israelite army. The Lord said to Joshua, "Each day for six days you and all your men shall walk once around the city walls. The Ark shall be carried behind you, led by seven priests holding trumpets made out of rams' horns. On the seventh day, you shall circle the city seven times, the priests shall blow their trumpets, and the people shout to the skies. Then will the walls of Jericho fall to the ground. All who live in the city will be killed except for Rahab and her family and household. They shall be spared, because it was she who hid our messengers."

And so it happened. Joshua warned his men not to make a sound for six days; but on the seventh day, as they walked for the seventh time around the city, Joshua said to his people, "Shout! For the Lord has given this city to you."

And so the Israelites raised a great shout, the priests blew their trumpets, and the walls of Jericho fell to the ground. Every man, woman, and child in the city was killed: only Rahab and those living in her house survived.

SHOFAR
Joshua's men would have steamed a ram's horn to make it soft, and then bent the wide end to form a trumpet, or *shofar*. The deep, mournful sounds of this horn are still heard in Jewish synagogues on certain holy days, such as the Day of Atonement, when the people think about the wrongs they have done.

The walls of Jericho fall to the ground

The Call of Gideon

THE ISRAELITES HAD A NEW AND POWERFUL ENEMY, the people of Midian. As soon as the grain was ready for harvest, the Midianites would attack, burning the wheat and slaughtering the animals. The Israelites had begun to worship other gods, but in their despair they appealed to God for help.

The Lord sent an angel to Gideon. "It is you who must save your people from this scourge," said the angel. Gideon, hot and tired from threshing the small amount of wheat he had managed to hide, looked at the angel in astonishment. "But I am only a poor farmer," he said.

"The Lord will be with you," the angel assured him.

That night, in obedience to God's word, Gideon smashed the altar that had been built to the god Baal. In its place he put up an altar to the Lord. The next morning the Israelites gathered around the fallen altar. "Who has done this terrible thing?" they demanded.

Soon it became known that Gideon was the man. "He must die!" shouted the crowd. But Gideon's father said, "If Baal is a god, then let

*Gideon
smashes the
altar of Baal*

*Gideon takes his men down to the
spring to drink, and chooses those
who are to fight with him*

12

him take his own revenge!" And to this the people agreed.

Gideon then gathered his forces and pitched camp by the spring of Harod. "If there are any among you who are afraid, let them go now," he commanded. At these words, over half his army of twenty-two thousand men turned for home. Then God told him to take the remaining ten thousand men down to the spring, and watch how they drank. God said to Gideon: "Those who cup the water in their hands, keep with you; but those who put their faces into the water, send away."

At last, with a company of only three hundred, Gideon looked down on the Midianite army camped in the valley below. When darkness fell, he gave each of his men a trumpet made of ram's horn and a flaming torch covered by an earthenware jar. Silently the army of Israelites surrounded the enemy camp, and at a signal from Gideon, blew their trumpets, smashed the jars to reveal the light from the torches, and shouted as loud as they could. Confused and terrified, the Midianites began fighting each other as they fled into the night.

So Gideon won his victory without striking a single blow.

SPRING OF HAROD
At God's command, Gideon watched to see how his soldiers drank from the waters of this spring. Those who cupped the water in their hands, rather than put their faces in the water, were chosen to fight. One interpretation is that God chose those who were the most alert and ready for battle.

Gideon's army attacks the Midianites at night

Samson and the Lion

OR FORTY YEARS the children of Israel had suffered at the hands of the Philistines, a fierce enemy from the lands near the sea. Then an angel appeared to an Israelite couple who had long been childless. "You will have a son who will win a great victory over the Philistines," the angel told them. "But you must be careful never to cut his hair." The angel then warned the woman. "While you are carrying the child, you must not touch wine or any strong drink, for your son will be a Nazirite, and his life will be dedicated to God."

LION
Lions were the most dangerous animals living in Canaan. They roamed wild in forests and thickets, and were a threat to other animals and people. Samson was so strong, he killed a lion with his bare hands.

Samson kills a lion, tearing it apart with his hands

The child was called Samson, and he grew tall and strong. One day Samson said to his father, "Father, I have seen a beautiful Philistine woman at Timnah, and I want her for my wife." His parents were unhappy that he had chosen a Philistine. "There are many Hebrew women who would make you a good wife: will you not look among them first?" But when they saw that Samson was determined, they did not stand in his way.

Samson and his parents went to Timnah, and as they walked through the vineyards a young lion leapt out at them. As easily as if he were swatting a fly, Samson killed it, tearing it apart with his hands. Then he went to the woman's house and they talked together, and she delighted Samson. It was not long before he asked her to marry him. A little later, he saw in the lion's carcass a honeycomb covered in bees; this he scooped out and ate as he walked, with no thought of being stung. He gave some to his parents, but did not say how he had come by it.

Samson eats honey, found in the lion's carcass

To celebrate his wedding he invited thirty of his wife's friends to a feast, which was to last seven days, for this was the custom of the country. On the first day, he put a riddle to his guests, promising rich rewards to anyone who could answer it. "Out of the eater comes meat; out of the strong comes sweet: what does this mean?" No one could guess. For three days they puzzled over it until finally one of the Philistines went to Samson's wife. "You must make your husband tell you the answer, or we will burn your house to the ground!"

Very frightened, Samson's wife went to him weeping. "How can you say you love me if you will not tell me the solution to your riddle? It is not much to ask!"

"I shall tell nobody," said Samson. "Not even you." But his wife coaxed and cried, until on the seventh day he told her. At once she ran to her friends with the news. And when that evening Samson again put the riddle, one of them stood up. "I can answer that!" he shouted. "There is nothing sweeter than honey. There is nothing stronger than a lion." Samson, realizing he had been tricked, was very angry. In his rage he killed thirty Philistines. Then he returned to his father's house and never saw his wife again.

BRAIDED HAIR
Samson was a Nazirite, a person dedicated to God. Nazirites had to promise never to cut their hair. Samson wore his uncut hair braided, like the prince in the stone sculpture above.

Samson and Delilah

Delilah ties Samson fast with seven bowstrings

She binds Samson with rope

She weaves Samson's long hair into the fabric of her loom

Delilah said to Samson,
"Tell me, I pray thee,
wherein thy great
strength lieth."
Judges 16:6

 Time passed, and Samson fell in love with a woman called Delilah. The Philistine lords went to Delilah and told her she must uncover the secret of Samson's great strength. "Find out how we may take him prisoner, and each one of us will give you eleven-hundred pieces of silver."

When Delilah was alone with Samson, she questioned him prettily.

"Tell me, what is the secret of your strength? And how could you be made captive?"

"If I were bound with seven new bowstrings, then I should be helpless as a child," Samson replied.

As if in play, Delilah then tied him fast with seven bowstrings given her by the Philistines, who were lying in wait in the next room. "The Philistines are upon us!" she cried. But Samson snapped the strings as easily as if they had been frail threads.

"Why did you not tell me the truth?" Delilah asked crossly.

"The truth?" said Samson. "The truth is that I can be held only by ropes that have never been used."

As before, Delilah bound him fast, and as before the Philistines burst in upon them, only to see Samson break the ropes as easily as if they had been spun of spider webs.

The third time Delilah put her question, Samson told her that if she wove his long hair into the fabric on her loom, then he would be

Weaving
In weaving, threads are intertwined to make cloth. This nomadic woman is weaving on a horizontal loom, similar to the one Delilah would have used.

weak. But again, when the Philistines tried to lay hands on him, he broke away effortlessly.

"How can you say you love me," sobbed Delilah, "when you tell me nothing but lies!" And she needled and nagged him until at last Samson, sick to death of her pestering, told his secret. "If my hair is cut, then my strength is gone."

PHILISTINE HEADDRESS
The Philistines lived along the Mediterranean coast in southwest Canaan from 1200 BC to 600 BC. They had a well-organized army. The soldiers wore distinctive feathered headdresses, as shown in the stone carving above, which made them appear very tall. They fought with iron swords and spears.

Delilah watches as the Philistines arrest Samson

Samson is led away in shackles

He fell asleep, exhausted, on her lap; and while he slept Delilah signaled to one of the Philistines, who crept in and cut off the strong man's hair. "Samson, the Philistines are upon us!" she cried. And Samson, not knowing that his strength had left him, jumped to his feet; but at once was overpowered.

His captors blinded him, and took him to Gaza where he was thrown into prison. There brass shackles were locked around his ankles, and he was put to work grinding wheat. But slowly his hair began to grow.

SAMSON TOLD DELILAH ALL HIS HEART, AND SAID UNTO HER, "THERE HATH NOT COME A RAZOR UPON MINE HEAD; FOR I HAVE BEEN A NAZIRITE UNTO GOD FROM MY MOTHER'S WOMB: IF I BE SHAVEN, THEN MY STRENGTH WILL GO FROM ME, AND I SHALL BECOME WEAK, AND BE LIKE ANY OTHER MAN."
JUDGES 16:17

Samson in the Temple

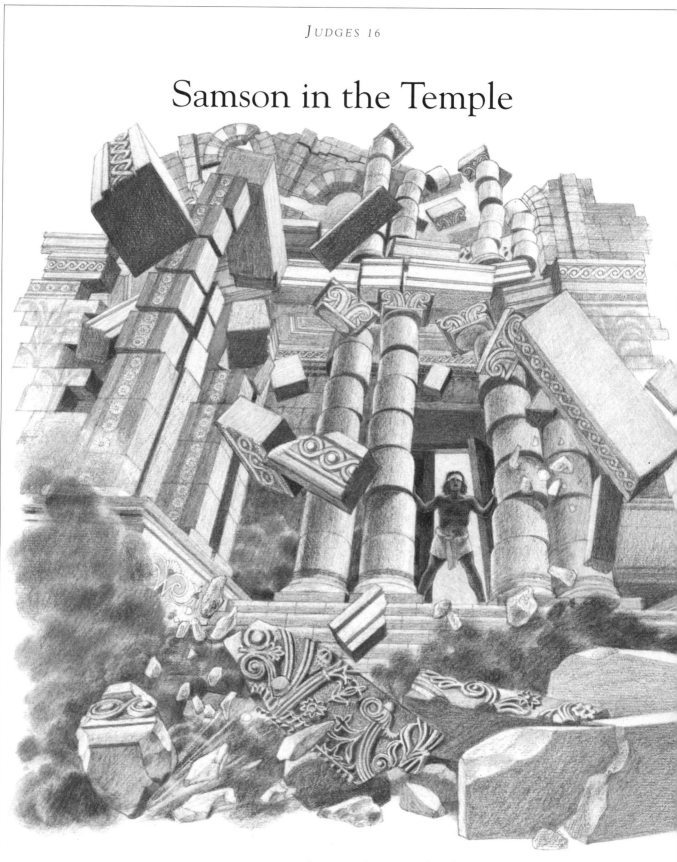

Samson pushes against the pillars of the temple

HE PHILISTINES WERE IN THE TEMPLE celebrating and offering sacrifices to their god, Dagon. "Thanks be to Dagon, for he has delivered the enemy into our hands!" they chanted. As the singing and dancing became louder and wilder, there were shouts for Samson.

"Bring him out! Let us see the Israelite champion! Where is his strength now!"

The blind prisoner was led into the temple and put to stand between the pillars of the doorway, so that everyone could see him. The crowd grew from hundreds to thousands, all of them laughing and jeering at Samson's helplessness.

"O Lord God, give me my strength once more!" Samson silently entreated.

Bracing his hands against the pillar on either side of him, Samson pushed with all his might. There was a noise as though the earth were cracking open, and suddenly the temple, roof and walls, crashed to the ground, killing everyone inside it, including Samson.

So, in dying, Samson won a final victory over the Philistines.

AND SAMSON CALLED UNTO THE LORD, AND SAID, "O LORD GOD, REMEMBER ME, I PRAY THEE, AND STRENGTHEN ME, I PRAY THEE, ONLY THIS ONCE, O GOD, THAT I MAY BE AT ONCE AVENGED OF THE PHILISTINES FOR MY TWO EYES."
JUDGES 16:28

The temple comes crashing down on the Philistines

Ruth and Naomi

Orpah returns to Moab, while Ruth and Naomi journey together to Bethlehem

Boaz watches Ruth working in his field

Orpah

Ruth

Naomi

BETHLEHEM
Ruth and Naomi would have traveled from Moab for about 50 miles (80 km) before reaching Bethlehem. The town is set high up on a hill and is surrounded by fertile fields. Bethlehem is the birthplace of David and Jesus.

OR MANY YEARS the widow Naomi had made her home in Moab. Her husband had died there, and so had her two sons. Their wives, Orpah and Ruth, lived with her. During a time of famine, Naomi decided to return to her own country, to Bethlehem. "We will come with you," said her daughters-in-law.

"No," said Naomi. "Your place is not with me, an old woman. You must stay in Moab where you belong."

Orpah was content with this, but Ruth loved Naomi and would not be parted from her. "Where you go, there shall I follow," she said. "Your home shall be mine; your people, my people; your God, my God." And so Ruth and Naomi journeyed together to Bethlehem.

They arrived at harvest time, and Ruth went into the fields to gather the leftover barley. Boaz, a cousin of Naomi's, who owned the fields, noticed the young woman and asked who she was. He was

*Ruth gathers
the barley that
is left over*

HARVESTING
The picture above shows
women cutting and
gathering grain during
harvest time. Poor
people, like Ruth, would
come later to collect any
leftover grain. This is
known as gleaning.

*While Boaz sleeps,
Ruth lies down at
his feet*

touched to hear about her
kindness to Naomi, and went over to
her. "Come and eat with us. You are safe
here with my people."

That evening Naomi told Ruth to return to Boaz. "Wait until he
has fallen asleep, then go quietly and lie down beside him."

As soon as she saw that Boaz slept, Ruth lay down at his feet. In the
middle of the night, he woke with a start and saw the form of a
woman in the darkness. "Who are you?"

"I am Ruth, and I have come to ask for your protection."

"There is someone closer to you in the family than I: but if he does
not wish to look after you and Naomi, then I shall take care of you."

And so it turned out. Ruth and Boaz were married, and Ruth gave
birth to a son, who brought great happiness to Naomi in her old age.

WHEN BOAZ HAD EATEN AND
DRUNK, AND HIS HEART WAS
MERRY, HE WENT TO LIE DOWN
AT THE END OF THE HEAP OF
WHEAT: AND SHE CAME
SOFTLY, AND UNCOVERED HIS
FEET, AND LAID HER DOWN.
RUTH 3:7

Samuel Is Called to Serve God

HANNAH WAS ONE of the two wives of Elkanah. Penninah had children, but even though Elkanah loved her, Hannah had none. Every year they went to pray at Shiloh, where the Ark of the Covenant was kept, and every year Penninah would mock Hannah because she had no children. One night Hannah went to the temple and prayed to God. "Lord, please send me a son, and I promise to devote his life to your service."

Eli, the high priest, watched her praying, then he blessed her as she left. "May God grant your wish," he said.

In due course Hannah gave birth to a son, whom she called Samuel.

BREASTPIECE
Eli was a high priest and would have worn a linen breastpiece like the one above. It is inset with 12 gemstones, representing the 12 tribes of Israel. The breastpiece was tied to an *ephod*, a two-piece apron, which the high priest wore over his blue robe.

Eli watches as Hannah prays to God for a son

Hannah gives her son, Samuel, to Eli to look after

TEACHING THE LAW
As a high priest, Eli would have taught Samuel to obey God's laws. In the same way, a rabbi – a teacher of Jewish laws – instructs the young today.

Hannah nursed the child, then, not forgetting her promise to God, she took Samuel to the temple and gave him to Eli to look after. Every year, when she came with her husband to pray at Shiloh, Hannah brought with her a little coat for Samuel. Eli cared for him lovingly and brought him up to obey God's word. The child grew as straight and true as Eli's own two sons were dishonest and sly.

One night Samuel was awakened by a voice calling his name. "Here I am," he said, and jumping from his bed ran to see what Eli wanted.

"I did not call you," said the old man. "Go back to bed."

But in a short while the boy heard the voice again – "Samuel, Samuel!" – and again he went in to Eli, but the priest assured him that he had not spoken. The third time Samuel heard the voice, Eli told him that it must be the voice of God.

So Samuel lay down in the dark and waited. "Samuel, Samuel."

"Lord," the child replied. "I am your servant, and ready to listen."

"The sons of Eli are evil men. You must tell their father that they cannot serve as priests or be pardoned for their wickedness."

The next morning Samuel told Eli what God had said. "So be it," said Eli. "It is the word of the Lord."

THE LORD CAME, AND STOOD, AND CALLED AS AT OTHER TIMES, "SAMUEL, SAMUEL." THEN SAMUEL ANSWERED, "SPEAK; FOR THY SERVANT HEARETH."
I SAMUEL 3:10

While Eli sleeps, Samuel is awakened by a voice calling him

Saul, the First King of the Israelites

Saul meets Samuel on a hill

Saul   Samuel

Samuel anoints Saul king

HORN AND OIL
Samuel anointed Saul king with oil contained in an animal's horn. It was a sign that Saul was chosen by God and belonged to the Lord in a special way. Samuel would have used olive oil, perfumed with spices and myrrh. The Israelites had many other uses for oil. They used it in cooking, to soothe cuts and bruises, for preparing a body for burial, and as fuel for lamps.

S AMUEL GREW OLD, and the people asked him to appoint a king to rule over them. Samuel asked God what he should do.

"There is a man called Saul, of the tribe of Benjamin, and he is the one you must choose. He will make himself known to you."

Shortly afterward, a tall young man came up to Samuel on a hill outside the city. "I have lost three of my donkeys," he said. "I know you are a prophet: can you tell me where they are?"

"Your donkeys are safe," Samuel replied. "Now come with me, for you are to be the first king of Israel." Saul was astonished. "But I am unimportant!" he exclaimed. "I am of the tribe of Benjamin, the smallest of all the tribes of Israel, and my family is the least important family in the tribe." Samuel reassured him, and led the astonished Saul back to his house, where he gave him food and then anointed him with oil, pouring it over his head.

"With this oil," he said, "I declare you king. Now you must return home. On your way you will see two men who will tell you your donkeys are found. Next you will meet three men, the first leading three young goats, the second carrying three loaves of bread, the third a bottle of wine; they will give you two of their loaves. Lastly, you will come across a group of prophets making music and singing praises to God, and you will join with them."

Everything happened exactly as predicted, after which Samuel called the children of Israel together. "I am here to show you your king," he told them. "Where is Saul, of the tribe of Benjamin?" But Saul, overwhelmed, was hiding among some baggage. He was soon found, however, and brought before Samuel, where he stood head and

SAMUEL SAID TO ALL THE PEOPLE, "SEE YE SAUL WHOM THE LORD HATH CHOSEN, THAT THERE IS NONE LIKE HIM AMONG ALL THE PEOPLE?" AND ALL THE PEOPLE SHOUTED, AND SAID, "LONG LIVE THE KING!"
I SAMUEL 10:24

Samuel calls the Israelites together and declares Saul king

shoulders taller than any man there.

"Here is your ruler!" said Samuel. "The man God has chosen to be your king."

And the people shouted, "Long live the king!"

Afterward Samuel wrote down the rules of kingship, dedicating his account to God. Then he told all the people – men, women, and children – to return to their homes.

Saul hides among baggage before he is found and brought before Samuel to become the first king of the Israelites

God Chooses David

GOD SPOKE TO SAMUEL, telling him to go to Bethlehem where he would find a man called Jesse. "I have chosen one of the sons of Jesse to be the next king," he said.

In Bethlehem, the news of Samuel's arrival made the people tremble, for he was now a great and powerful man. But Samuel

Jesse

Jesse's youngest son, David, watches over the sheep

Samuel

Samuel blesses seven of Jesse's sons, but knows that none of them has been chosen by God

reassured them. "I come in peace, to bless you and pray with you."

One by one, seven of Jesse's sons came to the prophet to be blessed. When Samuel saw the men standing before him, tall and handsome, he thought to himself, "Surely, one of these must be the chosen one." But as each of the brothers came before him in turn, he heard the Lord's voice, "This is not the man. God does not judge in the way people do. Do not look at the face but into the heart."

Finally, Samuel turned to Jesse and said, "God has chosen none of these men. Are all your children here?"

"All but the youngest, David, and he is out in the fields looking after the sheep."

"Fetch him," said Samuel.

The boy, fresh-faced and strongly built, came running in. "This is he," said God. Then Samuel took the holy oil and anointed David in front of his whole family. And from that day on the spirit of the Lord was with him.

SHEPHERD BOY
David was the youngest, and therefore the least important, of Jesse's sons. He looked after his father's sheep in the hills around Bethlehem. Out in all kinds of weather, his life would have been a lonely one as he led his sheep to good pasture, and protected them from harm. One story in the Bible tells how David risked his life by killing a bear and a lion that threatened the sheep.

Samuel anoints David the next king of the Israelites

David and Goliath

Saul's army gathers to do battle against the Philistines

David hurls a stone from his sling

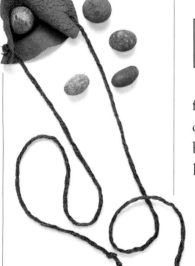

Slingshot
As a shepherd, David would have carried a sling for hurling stones at animals that threatened his sheep. The shepherd placed a stone in his pad, held the two ends of the sling, then swung it around at high speed. When he let go of one end, the stone would fly toward its target. Also used by soldiers, the sling was a deadly weapon.

THE PHILISTINES WERE READY for battle. On two hilltops, with only a narrow valley between, the armies were assembled, the Philistines on one, Saul and the Israelites on the other.

All of a sudden a giant man came striding down toward the valley from the Philistine camp. Goliath of Gath towered above everyone; on his head was a massive bronze helmet; he wore a breastplate of bronze, and his legs and arms were sheathed in bronze. In one hand he carried a bronze dagger, in the other an iron-headed spear as big as a tree.

"I challenge you, Saul!" bellowed Goliath. "I challenge you to send one of your men to fight me! Let the two of us decide the outcome of the war!"

At these words, Saul trembled, and the Israelites were filled with fear.

Three of Jesse's sons were among Saul's soldiers, and their brother David had left his sheep to bring them food. As he reached the camp, he heard Goliath's boastful challenge, and saw that no one dared answer it.

"I will fight the giant," he said to Saul.

"But you are only a boy. Goliath is a famous man of war."

Eventually, however, Saul was persuaded. Refusing both weapons and armor, David went to a nearby stream and picked out five smooth pebbles, which he put in his shepherd's pouch. Then, with his sling in

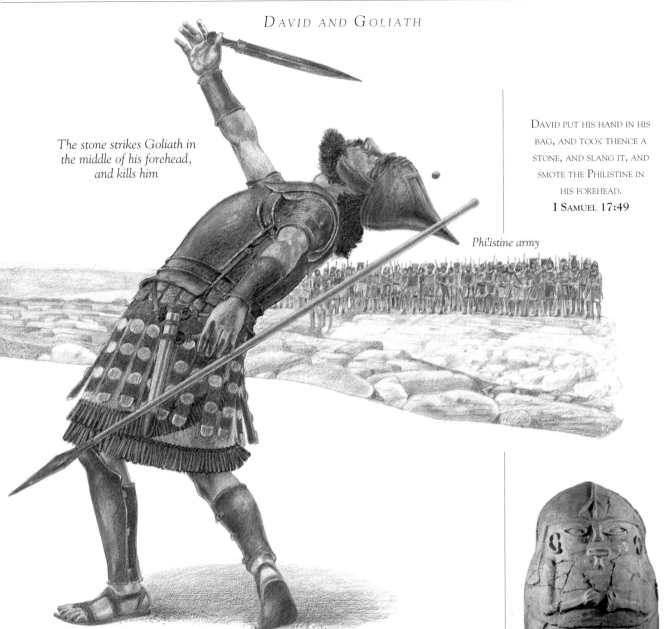

The stone strikes Goliath in the middle of his forehead, and kills him

DAVID PUT HIS HAND IN HIS BAG, AND TOOK THENCE A STONE, AND SLANG IT, AND SMOTE THE PHILISTINE IN HIS FOREHEAD.
I SAMUEL 17:49

Philistine army

PHILISTINE HEAD
The Philistines were one of the "Sea Peoples" who originally came from the islands in the Aegean Sea. They buried their dead in clay coffins, or sarcophagi. Strange-looking human features were engraved on the head ends of the coffins.

one hand, his staff in the other, he walked toward Goliath.

"Get out of my way, boy!" the champion shouted, his voice heavy with contempt. "I do not fight with children!"

"You come to me with a dagger and a spear, but I come to you with God on my side," said David. He put down his staff, and placed a pebble in his sling. Whirling it around once, he let it fly. The stone struck Goliath in the middle of his forehead, and the giant crashed to the ground, dead.

When the Philistines saw their great champion dead, they turned and ran, leaving the Israelites to celebrate their victory.

Long Live the King

JERUSALEM
Above is Jerusalem, also known as the "City of David," which became the Israelites' political and religious center. On the left is the Dome of the Rock, a Muslim mosque. It now stands on the site of Solomon's temple, which David made plans for and Solomon built.

DANCING FOR JOY
The picture above shows folk dancing in modern-day Syria. When the Israelites danced, it was a way of expressing their delight in God. On entering Jerusalem, the Israelites danced to thank God for their victory and to praise him.

IN THE TOWN OF HEBRON all the tribes of Israel gathered to proclaim David the new king of the Israelites. David took his people to Jerusalem, a city belonging to the Jebusites – for Jerusalem was to be his capital. But the Jebusites refused to open their gates, leaving the newcomers camped outside the walls.

However, some of David's men climbed up a waterpipe, which took them deep inside the city, and from there they were able to unlock the gates. Once inside, the Israelites defeated the Jebusites and captured the city.

The Ark of the Covenant was brought to Jerusalem, escorted by a crowd of thousands, singing and playing on pipes and tambourines.

The people escort the Ark into Jerusalem

As they entered the gates, trumpets sounded, and David took off his royal robes and danced for joy before the Ark of the Covenant.

When the Ark arrived at the ceremonial tent, or tabernacle, which had been built to house it, David offered burnt sacrifices to the Lord. Then he blessed his people, and gave everyone cakes and wine.

Michal, David's wife, watched him from a window as he mingled freely with the crowd. "How shameful to see the king of Israel dancing with the common people!" she said scornfully.

But David replied, "Nothing I do for the honor of God is shameful: the shame lies with those who despise me for it!" Then David resolved to build a temple in honor of the Lord.

MICHAL LOOKED THROUGH A WINDOW, AND SAW KING DAVID LEAPING AND DANCING BEFORE THE LORD; AND SHE DESPISED HIM IN HER HEART.
II SAMUEL 6:16

Michal watches David with scorn

tabernacle

Ark of the Covenant

David dances before the Ark

King Solomon's Wisdom

AND THE KING SAID, "BRING ME A SWORD." AND THEY BROUGHT A SWORD BEFORE THE KING. AND THE KING SAID, "DIVIDE THE LIVING CHILD IN TWO, AND GIVE HALF TO THE ONE, AND HALF TO THE OTHER."
I KINGS 3:24-25

Solomon orders that the baby be cut in two

One woman agrees with the order

The other woman pleads for her baby's life

HEN DAVID WAS DYING, he summoned his son, Solomon. "Soon I shall no longer be here to advise you," he said. "Always be strong and true, and always obey the word of God. If you do that, the Lord will be with you."

After David died, Solomon in his turn became king of Israel, and married the daughter of Pharaoh, king of Egypt, with whom he had made a treaty.

One night God appeared to him in a dream. "Ask for what you most want, and I will give it to you."

"You have made me king of a great people," Solomon replied. "But I have no more idea of how to govern than a child. Lord, give me wisdom."

Pleased with this answer, God said, "Because you asked nothing for yourself, neither for long life, nor wealth, nor victory over your enemies, I will grant your wish. If you do right and obey my laws, I will give you a wise and understanding heart, and you shall become known as a good king."

Soon afterward two women came before Solomon. They shared a house, and each had recently given birth to a child, but one child had died, and now both mothers were claiming the living baby as theirs.

"It is her baby who died," the first woman insisted. "Do you think I do not know my own child!"

"No, no!" cried the other. "It is her baby who is dead: in the night while I slept, she stole mine from my side!"

"Bring me my sword," said Solomon. The sword was brought. "Cut the child in two, and give half to each of the women standing here."

"Yes, O wise King, let neither of us have him," said one. "Cut him in two!"

But the other woman burst into tears and wrung her hands. "Do not kill my baby!" she cried. "I would rather give him away than have him hurt!" By this Solomon knew that she was the true mother, and he gave the child to her.

When the people heard of the judgment of Solomon they looked at their king with new respect, for they knew such wisdom could come to him only from God.

KING SOLOMON
Solomon was renowned for his wisdom, and this is shown in the story of the two women: he knew that the real mother would not agree to her baby being killed. The king wrote many wise sayings: most of the Book of Proverbs is thought to have been written by him. Under Solomon's rule the Israelites entered a golden age of peace and prosperity. This was crowned by the building of the temple, named after him, in Jerusalem.

The baby is given to the true mother

Solomon's Temple

NOW THAT THERE WAS peace at last, Solomon's greatest wish was to carry out the plan of his father, David, to build a temple for the worship of God. He sent word to Hiram, king of Tyre, asking him for wood from the great cedars of Lebanon. The huge trees were felled, then roped to rafts and floated down the coast. At the same time thousands of laborers quarried and cut the stones for the foundations and outer walls of the temple.

It took four years to lay the foundations, and three to build the temple upon them. Inside the temple, the walls were of cedarwood, carved with flowers and trees and painted with gold. The altar, too, was covered in gold.

When it was finished, Solomon, accompanied by the priests and tribal leaders, brought the Ark of the Covenant to the temple, where it was placed carefully in the inner sanctuary.

Suddenly the temple was filled with a cloud, so the priests could not carry out their duties. It was the glory of God filling the house of the Lord.

CEDARS OF LEBANON
Large, evergreen cedar trees covered the hills of Lebanon in Solomon's time. Cedarwood was valued for its beauty, fragrance, and strength.

SOLOMON'S TEMPLE
Solomon's temple replaced the tabernacle, or sacred tent, in providing a permanent home for the Ark of the Covenant. The Ark, flanked by two golden cherubim, was placed in the innermost room, the Holy of Holies. The temple was at the center of the Israelites' faith because it was the place where God was (see page 17).

Laborers cut the stones for the temple

It takes seven years to build Solomon's temple

Winged cherubim are carved for the inside of the temple

CARVED IVORY
Cherubim, winged
creatures, were carved on
the inside of the temple.
They may have looked
like this sphinx from
Nimrud in Assyria.

35

The Queen of Sheba

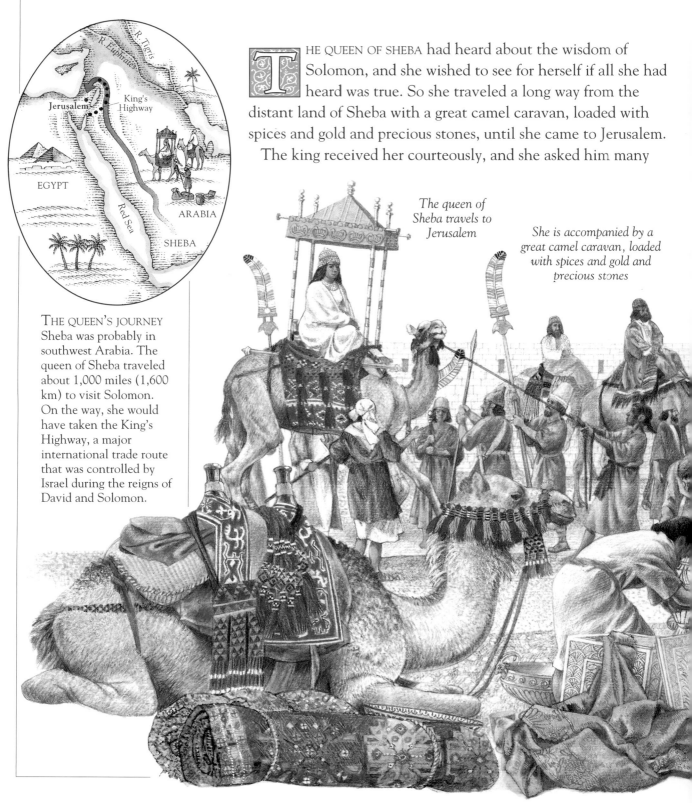

THE QUEEN OF SHEBA had heard about the wisdom of Solomon, and she wished to see for herself if all she had heard was true. So she traveled a long way from the distant land of Sheba with a great camel caravan, loaded with spices and gold and precious stones, until she came to Jerusalem. The king received her courteously, and she asked him many

The queen of Sheba travels to Jerusalem

She is accompanied by a great camel caravan, loaded with spices and gold and precious stones

THE QUEEN'S JOURNEY
Sheba was probably in southwest Arabia. The queen of Sheba traveled about 1,000 miles (1,600 km) to visit Solomon. On the way, she would have taken the King's Highway, a major international trade route that was controlled by Israel during the reigns of David and Solomon.

difficult questions. But none was too difficult for Solomon: he answered them all.

Then she looked around her, at his servants and his ministers, at his magnificent golden palace and happy, prosperous people, and she knew that here was a man both wise and good. "I would not believe it, until I had seen with my own eyes," she said. "Israel is fortunate in its king."

She gave Solomon many magnificent gifts, while he in his turn presented her with everything her heart desired. His wealth and generosity were without limit, and the queen returned to her own country laden with the riches of Israel.

King Solomon comes out from his palace to receive the queen

PRECIOUS GIFTS
Sheba became a wealthy land by trading spices, gold, and jewels. When the queen of Sheba visited King Solomon and brought expensive gifts with her, she may have wished to make a trade agreement with the king.

AFRICAN QUEEN
Legend has it that the queen of Sheba ruled over Ethiopia and Egypt.

Elijah in the Wilderness

TWO KINGDOMS
Solomon, who belonged to the tribe of Judah, had not always treated the northern tribes well. When Rehoboam became king these tribes rebelled. The kingdom was then split into two: Israel, with Samaria as its capital, in the north; Judah, with Jerusalem as its capital, in the south.

AFTER THE DEATH of Solomon, his son Rehoboam became king. There was unrest among the tribes in the north, but Rehoboam did not listen to the people's troubles. The tribes rebelled and the kingdom was split in two, into Israel and Judah. Then, the people of Israel turned against God. The times were so wicked that the prophet Elijah foretold there would be a drought lasting many years.

The Lord spoke to Elijah. "Go to the stream that runs in the valley of Kerith, and live there in secret. You can drink from the brook, and the ravens will bring you food." And indeed every morning and evening ravens appeared with bread and meat in their beaks; but soon the stream dried up from the lack of rain.

In obedience to God, Elijah then went to the city of Sidon, where he met a woman gathering sticks

Elijah drinks from the brook and is fed by ravens

*Elijah brings the woman's
son back to life*

outside the city walls. "Please, give me something to eat," Elijah asked her.

"I have nothing but a jar of flour and a little oil," she said. "And with that I must feed myself and my son, or we will starve."

"Go to your house, and there you will find enough flour and enough oil to last until the rains come." And it happened just as the prophet said. There was food every day for the woman, her son, and for Elijah.

But then the woman's son fell ill and died. "Do you call yourself a man of God!" she cried to Elijah. "You, who have let God take my son from me!" Elijah gently lifted up the boy, laid him on his own bed, and three times he bent over him.

"O Lord," he prayed. "Let this child's life return." And in a short while the boy took a deep breath, opened his eyes, and sat up. Elijah lifted the child and brought him to his mother, who was overjoyed. "Now I know you are truly a man of God," she said.

RAVENS
According to Old Testament law, a raven was unclean and could not be sacrificed or eaten. In spite of this, God sent ravens to bring food to Elijah in the desert, showing that the most humble can serve God.

Elijah's Final Journey

Elisha

Elijah beats the surface of the River Jordan with his cloak and the waters divide

ONE DAY ELIJAH WAS TRAVELING WITH ELISHA, whom he had chosen to be his successor. Elijah, knowing that he was soon to die, asked Elisha to go with him no farther. Elisha loved the older man, and wanted to stay with him. "I shall not leave you," he said. So the two men continued on their way.

At Bethel, Elijah again turned to Elisha. "You must stay here, while I go on alone." But still Elisha would not leave him.

Finally, they came to the River Jordan. Elijah took off his cloak and beat the surface of the water with it. The waters divided, and the prophets crossed the river, walking on a pathway of dry land.

Suddenly a chariot of fire appeared out of the sky, drawn by horses flaming scarlet and gold. Before Elisha knew what was happening, Elijah was whirled up into the chariot, which, with the sound of a shrieking, rushing wind, disappeared from sight. Elisha, staring up into the clouds, cried out in wonder. But Elijah was never seen again.

Slowly Elisha took up Elijah's cloak and hit the surface of the river, calling on God to help him. The waters parted and he walked to the other side on dry land. The spirit of Elijah was now with him.

Elijah is whirled up into the skies in a chariot of fire

CHARIOT OF GOLD
Above is a gold model of a chariot pulled by four horses. It dates from around 500 BC. In ancient times, chariots were used in warfare and in ceremonies. In battle, a chariot usually carried two men: a driver who held the reins; and a warrior who carried a bow and arrow or a spear.

Elisha takes up Elijah's cloak

Elisha and the Woman of Shunem

O N HIS TRAVELS ELISHA often visited the city of Shunem. In the city lived a rich woman who invited him to eat with her and her husband every time he passed by. The woman said that Elisha could stay whenever he wished, and made ready a little room for him on the roof, with a bed, a table, a stool, and a lamp.

One evening as Elisha lay on his bed, he called his servant, Gehazi. "How can I repay the kindness of this woman?" he asked.

"I know that what she wants most is a child," Gehazi replied. "But her husband is too old to father children."

"Ask her to come here," said Elisha. The woman came, and stood in the doorway to hear what Elisha had to say.

"Soon," he told her, "you will have a son."

"No, that cannot be," she protested. But just as the prophet said, within a year she gave birth to a boy.

ELISHA
The painting above is of the prophet Elisha. When Elisha took up Elijah's cloak, it symbolized that he was chosen by God to succeed Elijah as the prophet of Israel. In the Bible, Elisha is described as being bald-headed, and once he was mocked by some children for his baldness. Two bears then appeared and attacked the children.

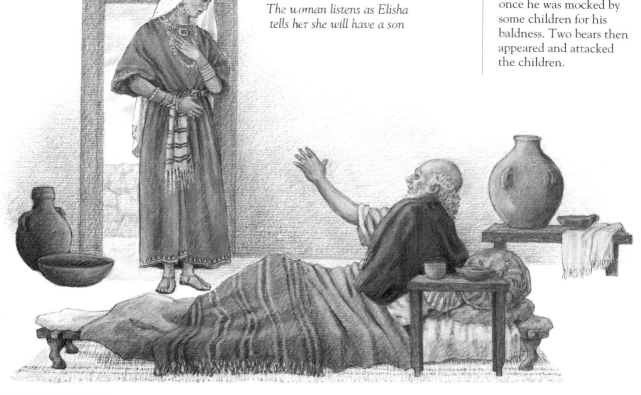

The woman listens as Elisha tells her she will have a son

*The servant carries the sick boy back to
the house and gives the child to his mother,
but by midday he is dead*

SHUNEM
The town of Shunem,
present day Solem, lies in
the fertile Jezreel Valley.
The town is about 3
miles (5 km) north of the
town of Jezreel, near
Mount Gilboa. Shunem
was situated on a well-
used route, which
explains why Elisha often
visited the town.

When the boy was older, he went out one morning to find his
father who was harvesting in the fields. "Father, help me! There
is a pain in my head which I cannot bear!" Frightened by his
son's appearance, his father told a servant to carry him at once
to the house. There his mother took him and held him on her
lap, but by midday he was dead. With tears running down her
cheeks, she carried the lifeless body to Elisha's room, laid it on
the bed, and closed the door.

"Quickly!" she said to her husband. "Fetch a donkey, and let me
have a servant to accompany me. I am going to find Elisha."

Traveling as fast as they could, they soon caught up with the
prophet at Mount Carmel. Dismounting, the woman clutched Elisha's
feet, but Gehazi pushed her away. "Leave her alone," Elisha said. "She
is in distress, and I must know what is wrong." As soon as the woman
had spoken, Elisha said to Gehazi, "Take my staff and, girding your
loins, run as fast as you can to Shunem. Go to the boy, and touch his
face with the staff. I and the boy's mother will follow you."

Gehazi did as his master had said. On entering the house, he
touched the boy's face with the staff, but the body remained still

and cold. "The boy is dead," he whispered sadly as Elisha arrived. Elisha went alone to the room in which the body lay. Closing the door behind him, he knelt and prayed to God. Then very carefully he lay down on top of the child, putting his mouth to the boy's mouth, his eyes against his eyes, his hands against the dead boy's hands. As he did so he felt the flesh beneath him grow warm. Elisha stood up and watched as the color returned to the face of what only minutes ago had been a lifeless body.

After the boy's mother has found Elisha, they travel back to Shunem together

Elisha's servant, Gehazi, runs on ahead with Elisha's staff in his hand

Suddenly the boy sneezed, and sneezed again. Then he opened his eyes and sat up.

"Come and embrace your son!" Elisha called. The woman ran into the room and gasped. Falling on her knees before the prophet, she thanked him with all her heart. Then, hand in hand, she and her son left the room together.

GIRDED LOINS
Gehazi "girded his loins" when he ran to Shunem. This means that he would have put his robe between his legs and tucked it into his belt, like the Syrian workman shown in the picture. Laborers often did this to give them greater freedom of movement when they were working.

ELISHA WENT UP, AND LAY UPON THE CHILD, AND PUT HIS MOUTH UPON HIS MOUTH, AND HIS EYES UPON HIS EYES, AND HIS HANDS UPON HIS HANDS: AND HE STRETCHED HIMSELF UPON THE CHILD; AND THE FLESH OF THE CHILD WAXED WARM.
II KINGS 4:34

Elisha brings the boy back to life

Elisha and Naaman

king of Israel

AAMAN, THE COMMANDER OF THE SYRIAN ARMY, was a brave and clever soldier, but for some years he had suffered from the skin disease of leprosy. Namaan's wife had recently taken as a maid a young Israelite who had been captured in battle.

Naaman presents a letter to the king of Israel, asking to be cured of his leprosy

Naaman

SYRIAN KING
This ivory figure of a Syrian king is thought to be Hazael, who fought against the Israelites around the time of Elisha.

The girl said to her mistress, "How I wish my master could go to the prophet Elisha, who is in Samaria, for I know he could cure him!"

This was repeated to Naaman, who went at once to the king of Syria. "Of course you must go," said the king. "I myself will write a letter on your behalf to the king of Israel, asking that your leprosy be treated." And so Naaman set off, taking with him the letter and a splendid collection of gifts: ten talents of silver, six thousand pieces of gold, and ten complete sets of richly embroidered clothing.

When Naaman presented the king of Syria's letter, the king of Israel was angry. "Am I expected to work miracles?" he demanded. "This is only an excuse for Syria to quarrel with us yet again!"

Naaman

Naaman drives up to
Elisha's door in his chariot

Elisha's messenger tells
Naaman to go and
bathe seven times in the
River Jordan

RIVER JORDAN
The River Jordan was the
longest and most
important river in
Canaan. "Jordan" means
"flowing downward": the
river begins at Lake
Huleh in the north and
flows down to the Sea of
Galilee. From there it
drops lower until it
reaches the Dead Sea.
The distance from the
Sea of Galilee to the
Dead Sea is 70 miles (113
km), but the river winds
so much that it is more
than twice that long.

Elisha heard what had happened and he sent word to the court. "Let
Naaman come to me," he said, "and his wish shall be granted." When
Naaman drove up to Elisha's door with his chariot and horses, Elisha
remained inside, sending a messenger in his place. "The prophet says
you must go down to the River Jordan and bathe seven times in the
water. Then you will be cured."

Naaman was outraged. "Why did Elisha himself not speak to me?
All he had to do was touch me with his hand and I would have been
healed! And why the Jordan? We have greater rivers in my own land."
In a fury he turned to leave, but one of his servants stopped him.

"Master," he said. "If the prophet had asked of you some difficult
task, you would have done it without question. But all he
requires is that you bathe in the River Jordan: should you
not agree to this simple instruction?"

Realizing the sense in the man's words, Naaman went down to
the river and immersed himself seven times in the water. When
he stepped out on the bank after the seventh time, he saw that
his skin, which had been covered in sores, was as smooth
and clean as a child's.

Overcome with joy, he returned to Elisha to thank
him. "Now I know that there is no god but the God of
Israel!" He begged Elisha to accept the magnificent
presents he had brought with him from Syria. Elisha
refused his gifts, but blessed him and sent him on his way.

Naaman is healed in the River Jordan

Jonah and the Great Fish

SPERM WHALE
The "fish" that swallowed Jonah may have been a sperm whale. These whales are known to visit the eastern Mediterranean Sea. With their large throats, they can swallow the body of a man whole.

OD TOLD HIS PROPHET, Jonah, to go to Nineveh, and warn the people there to turn away from their wickedness. But Jonah disliked the Ninevites and did not want them to hear God's message, so he went instead to Joppa. There he found a berth on a ship sailing to Tarshish. As soon as the ship put out to sea, God sent a great wind that whipped the water up into a storm, and it seemed that the ship would break apart. The sailors, terrified, threw everything they could overboard to lighten the load.

The captain went below, where he found Jonah fast asleep. "Wake up, and pray to your God to save us!" he cried. Meanwhile, the sailors on deck were drawing lots to discover who among them was the cause of the storm. The name drawn was Jonah's.

"Yes," he said. "I am the cause of the trouble. I am an Israelite, and I ran away from the Lord. Throw me over the side, and the storm will die down." At first the men hesitated, and tried to row the ship toward the shore, but the waves grew

The sailors throw Jonah overboard

Jonah is swallowed by a giant fish and for three days and three nights he remained in its belly

higher and the wind screamed louder, and they took hold of Jonah and threw him into the sea. At once the wind dropped and the water grew calm.

As Jonah swam in the sea, he was swallowed by a giant fish. For three days and nights he remained in its belly, praying to God and thanking the Lord for keeping him alive, until the fish vomited Jonah onto dry land.

Again the Lord told Jonah to go to Nineveh, and this time he went, and warned the people that their city would be destroyed. The king and all his subjects, knowing that they had done wrong, begged God to spare them and promised that they would mend their ways. God heard their prayers and resolved not to harm them.

Jonah, however, was angry that the city was to be spared.

The fish vomits Jonah onto dry land

As Jonah watches over Nineveh, God makes a vine grow to shade him from the sun, but then causes it to wither and die

He built himself a shelter outside the city walls, meaning to stay there until Nineveh fell. God, watching over him, made a vine grow up to shade Jonah from the sun. But the next morning God sent a worm that fed on the roots of the vine until it withered and died. The sun grew hot, and a stifling wind blew from the east, until Jonah was suffering so much he wished himself dead. "Why are you angry that the vine has withered?" God asked him. "Why do you care about a vine that you neither planted nor watered, while you resent my care for the well-being of a city of thousands of souls?"

NINEVEH
Above is a model of part of the wall that once surrounded Nineveh, the capital of Assyria. The wall was 8 miles (13 km) long. Parks and many grand buildings once lay within these walls.

The Prophet Isaiah

ISAIAH WAS A PROPHET of the Lord. Through him God spoke to the people. Isaiah warned them what would happen if they failed to obey God's commandments; he told them, too, of the coming of the Messiah, who would bring hope and the chance of salvation to everyone on earth.

One day in the temple in Jerusalem, Isaiah had a vision. He saw God high up on a throne. God's robes were so vast that they swirled and billowed into every corner of the temple. Above were the seraphs: each had six wings, two to cover his face, two to cover his feet, and two to fly. Continuously they sang, "Holy, holy, holy is the Lord!" And at the sound of their voices the chamber shook to its foundations and the room was filled with smoke.

"When I hear these words," Isaiah cried, "I know how unclean are the words that come from my mouth!" As he spoke he saw one of the seraphs take a red-hot coal from the altar and fly toward him. The seraph touched Isaiah's lips with the burning coal, and said, "Now your guilt is burned away and you are without sin."

Then he heard God saying, "Who can I send?"

Isaiah replied, "Here am I: send me."

"You must take my message to the people," said the Lord. "But you will find that at first they will not listen or understand, and they will refuse to be healed."

Isaiah was saddened by God's message. But throughout his life he continued to listen to the word of God. His spirits rose when he heard tell of the time to come, when happiness and joy will be everywhere. The desert will flower, the weak become strong, the lame man leap like a deer. The Lord will walk in the wilderness. God will come down to earth to tend to the people as lovingly as a shepherd tends his lambs, giving them food and water and protecting them from evil. Those who follow in the way of the Lord will be given new strength, and will be safe forever after.

Isaiah sees a vision in the temple

HE SHALL FEED HIS FLOCK LIKE A SHEPHERD: HE SHALL GATHER THE LAMBS WITH HIS ARM, AND CARRY THEM IN HIS BOSOM, AND SHALL GENTLY LEAD THOSE THAT ARE WITH YOUNG.
ISAIAH 40:11

Hezekiah's Gold

THE KING OF ASSYRIA swept through Israel with his army, slaying all who stood in his way, burning crops, laying siege to cities, and taking prisoner anyone who did not escape.

This terrible punishment had fallen on the children of Israel because they had disobeyed the Lord. In recent years they had grown greedy and corrupt; they had ignored the warnings of the prophets, and returned to worshiping false gods. And now their country was occupied, and the ten tribes were forced to work as slaves.

In time a new king ascended the throne of Judah. Hezekiah was not only a wise ruler but a good man who obeyed God's laws. He destroyed the pagan altars and insisted that his people keep the ten commandments. A brave warrior, he had won many victories against his enemies, but not even he could withstand the might of King Sennacherib of Assyria.

Desperate to stop the invaders, Hezekiah sent word to Sennacherib, begging him to withdraw his army. "If you agree to leave my land," he said, "I will pay any price you name."

The Assyrian king demanded huge sums in silver and gold, and in order to find them the precious metals were stripped from the very walls and pillars of the temple. Sennacherib kept the treasure, but broke his promise to go, ordering his soldiers to attack Jerusalem itself. Once the city was surrounded, he sent a message demanding that Hezekiah surrender.

Not knowing where else to turn, Hezekiah went to the temple to pray and ask for help from the prophet Isaiah. "Do not be afraid," said Isaiah. "God will defend you and save the city."

That night the angel of death flew low over the Assyrian camp, leaving many hundreds of thousands dead. In the morning instead of an army, Sennacherib saw only rows and rows of bodies. Turning his back on Jerusalem, he made his way home to Nineveh.

HEZEKIAH'S TUNNEL
King Hezekiah once ordered that a tunnel be dug beneath Jerusalem, so that the city's water supply would not be cut off by the invading Assyrians. Today, water still flows through Hezekiah's Tunnel.

Silver and gold are stripped from the temple

Jeremiah and the Potter's Wheel

GOD SPOKE TO A YOUNG MAN called Jeremiah, telling him that he had been chosen as a prophet. "But I am young," said Jeremiah, "and know nothing!"

"Do not be afraid," said the Lord, "for I am with you."

Then God's hand touched the man's mouth. "Now I have put words into your mouth. Tell me, what do you see?"

"I see the branch of an almond tree in bloom."

"Yes, you are right. I am watching to see that my word is fulfilled. What else do you see?"

"I see a boiling cauldron on the fire, tilted toward the north."

"It is from the north that disaster will come, a terrible punishment that will fall upon the land of Judah. For my people have forgotten me, and they worship false gods. You must speak to them, Jeremiah, tell them what I intend. They will turn on you, but you need fear nothing while I am with you!"

Then God sent Jeremiah to the house of a potter, who was at work at his wheel. Jeremiah watched the clay take shape; but the potter saw the shape was lopsided, and taking the wet clay in his hands, squeezed and molded it until he had made the jar perfect.

"Israel is like clay in my hands," said the Lord. "If my people persist in doing evil, they will be destroyed. But if they repent, I will make of them something good and strong. Go, Jeremiah, and tell them this."

The prophet did as God had said. He bought a clay jar; then he summoned the priests and wise men, and led them into the valley of Ben Hinnom.

"You will suffer war, famine, and plague unless you give up worshiping Baal and all your other false gods!" he told them.

In the silence that followed, Jeremiah lifted up the clay jar and hurled it to the ground so that it shattered into a thousand pieces. "Just as I have destroyed this jar, so will God

ALMOND TREE
The almond was the first tree to blossom in the spring. Its nuts were used for making oil. Just as Jeremiah is watching the almond tree, God is watching the world. The Hebrew for "watching" is similar to "almond tree."

Jeremiah watches a potter shaping clay at his wheel

Jeremiah hurls a clay jar to the ground

He tells the priests and the wise men that just as he has destroyed the jar, so will God destroy the wicked Judeans

destroy the people of Judah if they do not listen to the Lord's word!"

But the Judeans did not listen, and the day soon came when Jeremiah's prophesy was fulfilled. Nebuchadnezzar, king of Babylon, sent a great army to attack Jerusalem. The city was taken and many of its people were led in chains to Babylon. Nebuchadnezzar chose a new king, Zedekiah, to rule Judah. Zedekiah had to obey the Babylonian king if Jerusalem were to be left in peace.

"Now what do you see?" the Lord asked Jeremiah.

"I see two baskets of figs set down outside the temple. One basket is full of figs that are ripe and juicy, the other full of bruised, rotten fruit that no one would want to eat."

"The Judeans in Babylon are like the ripe figs: they will repent of their sins, and I will bring them out of captivity and look after them well. But King Zedekiah and those Judeans who stayed in Jerusalem will not repent. They are rotten to the core, and nowhere shall they ever find rest or prosperity."

The ripe figs are like the repentant Judeans, while the rotten figs are like those who do not repent

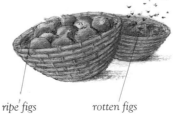

ripe figs   rotten figs

POTTER
Pottery is an ancient craft. This Egyptian figure of a potter at his wheel dates from around 2500 BC. Potters "threw" their clay pots on a wooden or stone wheel. They placed the clay on the wheel, then turned the wheel with their hand or feet as they molded the clay. God compared his control over people to the potter's control of clay.

The Israelites in Captivity

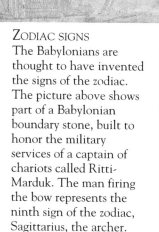

Jeremiah is lowered into a pit by King Zedekiah's men

YEARS PASSED, and the prophet Jeremiah, knowing that Jerusalem was in terrible danger, tried to warn the people. "You will die if you remain here," he said. "Soon the city will be in the hands of the Babylonians, and only those who leave now will survive."

Among those listening were some army officers, and they complained bitterly about Jeremiah to Zedekiah, king of Jerusalem. "It is not for me to interfere," said Zedekiah. "You must do with him as you choose." So the officers seized the prophet, and lowered him by a rope into a deep, dark pit, whose stone floor was thickly covered in mud. There was nothing in the pit either to eat or drink. Ebed-Melech, a member of the royal household, discovered what

The king relents, and Jeremiah is hauled to the surface

ZODIAC SIGNS
The Babylonians are thought to have invented the signs of the zodiac. The picture above shows part of a Babylonian boundary stone, built to honor the military services of a captain of chariots called Ritti-Marduk. The man firing the bow represents the ninth sign of the zodiac, Sagittarius, the archer.

had happened, and knew that Jeremiah would die if left in captivity. He went at once to the king, who agreed to the prisoner's release.

Ebed-Melech went with thirty men to the dungeon with ropes and a pile of old rags. These he threw down to Jeremiah. "Put the ropes under your arms, and bind them with these rags so that the rope will not hurt you." Then they hauled Jeremiah slowly to the surface.

But still Jeremiah's warnings were ignored. Within a short while Nebuchadnezzar, king of Babylon, laid siege to the city. For two years the enemy army surrounded the walls, so that no one could go in or out. The people were sick and starving, and at last in despair they threw open the gates, and Nebuchadnezzar took possession of Jerusalem.

Zedekiah, meanwhile, had fled with a small group of men, but he was soon captured. His sons were killed in front of him, Zedekiah's eyes were put out, and he was led in chains like a slave to Babylon.

On Nebuchadnezzar's orders, the temple and the royal palace and many houses were set on fire, and the city walls razed to the ground. People were rounded up and taken away – only the poor and weak were left behind to scratch what living they could from vineyards and fields.

ISHTAR GATE
This is a detail from the Ishtar Gate, built during King Nebuchadnezzar's reign of Babylon. Its enameled bricks were decorated with lions and bulls.

The Babylonians take possession of Jerusalem and King Zedekiah is led away in chains

Jerusalem is set on fire

The Israelites are rounded up and taken to Babylon

THEY SLEW THE SONS OF ZEDEKIAH BEFORE HIS EYES, AND PUT OUT THE EYES OF ZEDEKIAH, AND BOUND HIM WITH FETTERS OF BRASS, AND CARRIED HIM TO BABYLON.
II KINGS 25:7

The Golden Statue

Daniel tells King Nebuchadnezzar the meaning of his dreams, and in return the king gives Daniel and his three friends important posts

NEBUCHADNEZZAR, king of Babylon, was tormented by bad dreams. He consulted wise men, astrologers, and magicians, but none could tell him what his dreams conveyed. Eventually the king lost patience, and threatened them all with death, but still none was found who could interpret the terrible image of his nightmare.

Among the wise men was Daniel, a Judean who had been captured by the Babylonians. He was one of a group of young noblemen of exceptional intelligence, strength of character, and good looks who had been chosen for special training. They had been taught the language and history of Babylon, and after three years had been taken into the king's service. With Daniel were three others from Judah who were given new names by their captors: Shadrach, Meshach, and Abednego. The four men soon became good friends. They were all clever and quick to learn, but Daniel had a special gift: he was able to interpret dreams.

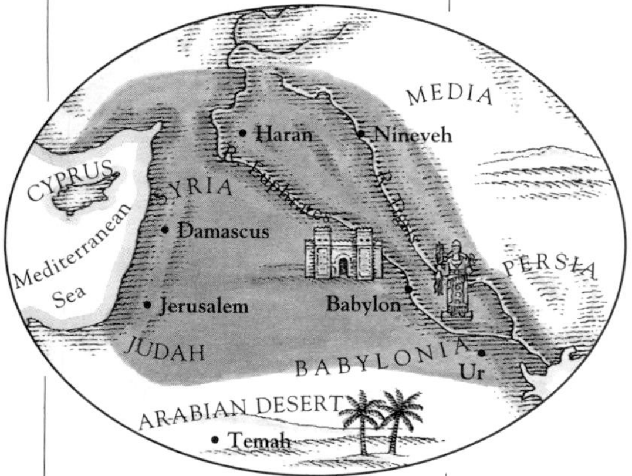

BABYLONIAN EMPIRE
Under King Nebuchadnezzar II (605-562 BC), the Babylonian empire expanded until it dominated the ancient Middle East. The Judeans were one of the peoples that were conquered by the Babylonians and moved far from their homeland.

Having been sentenced to death with the others, Daniel went to see the king. "Please, sire, let us have more time. I am sure that I will soon be able to tell you the meaning of your dreams," To this Nebuchadnezzar assented, and Daniel and his three friends prayed to God for help. That night God revealed the secret of the king's dream.

Next day, Daniel went again to Nebuchadnezzar. "God has done what your wise men could not, and shown me the meaning of your dreams.

"As you slept, you saw a gigantic statue towering above you. Its head was sculpted of pure gold, its chest and arms of silver, its belly and thighs of bronze, its legs of iron, and its feet part iron, part clay. Suddenly a stone smashed against the statue's feet, and shattered them – whereupon the entire structure, gold, silver, and bronze, crashed to the ground, reduced to nothing but particles of dust. The wind blew the dust away, and the stone became a great mountain that covered the whole earth.

"I will tell you the meaning of this," said Daniel. "The statue's head of gold represents you, great King, and the parts made of silver, bronze, iron, and clay are the empires which shall come after yours, some strong, some weak and easily divided, none lasting forever. The stone is the kingdom of God; it is greater than any kingdom on Earth, and shall never be destroyed."

Nebuchadnezzar was so impressed with Daniel's wisdom that he knelt before him, swearing allegiance to his God. Loading him with treasure, he appointed Daniel governor of Babylon and chief of all his advisers. He also gave important posts to Daniel's friends, Shadrach, Meshach, and Abednego.

Later, the king gave orders for a statue to be built, ninety feet high, nine feet wide, and made of solid gold. He had it set upon the plain of Dura, and with great pomp and ceremony commanded all his officers, governors, captains, and counselors to come and worship the statue as a god. Only Daniel's three friends refused.

When Nebuchadnezzar learned that his order had been defied, he flew into a rage, and demanded that Shadrach, Meshach, and Abednego be brought before him. "If you do not worship as I tell you," shouted the king, "I will have you thrown into a fiery furnace and burnt to death!"

The king orders that a statue made of solid gold be built and commands everyone to worship the statue

THEN NEBUCHADNEZZAR
CAME NEAR TO THE MOUTH OF
THE BURNING FIERY FURNACE,
AND SPAKE, AND SAID,
"SHADRACH, MESHACH, AND
ABEDNEGO, YE SERVANTS OF
THE MOST HIGH GOD, COME
FORTH, AND COME HITHER."
THEN SHADRACH, MESHACH,
AND ABEDNEGO CAME FORTH
OF THE MIDST OF THE FIRE.

DANIEL 3:26

The three men quietly replied, "We will not worship your statue, but our God will save us from the furnace, and protect us even from you, great King. We have nothing to fear."

Nebuchadnezzar, beside himself with rage, had the furnace heated to seven times its usual heat. Then the men, fully clothed, were thrown into the flames. But as he watched, Nebuchadnezzar saw to his astonishment that the three men walked through the fire unharmed, and that beside them stood an unknown fourth man.

"Shadrach, Meshach, and Abednego, come out of the furnace," said the king, his voice full of awe. As they stepped from the flames, everyone saw that not a hair was singed, not a thread of clothing was burnt. Nebuchadnezzar took each in turn by the hand. "From this day, the Jewish people may worship their God, who sent his angel to rescue these men," he vowed. "And I will decree that my people, too, shall worship only your God." Then he embraced the three friends, and gave them positions of great power in the government of Babylon.

The three friends walk through the fire unharmed, while beside them stands an unknown fourth man

King Nebuchadnezzar calls to the three men to come out of the furnace

Belshazzar's Feast

*King Belshazzar suddenly sees before him
a hand, writing on the plaster of the wall*

King Belshazzar

BELSHAZZAR, THE NEW KING OF BABYLON, gave a great feast. He gave orders that the gold and silver cups which his father, Nebuchadnezzar, had plundered from the temple in Jerusalem, should be used as goblets for wine.

As Belshazzar and his friends shouted and laughed and drank toasts to their gods, suddenly they saw before them a hand writing on the white plaster of the wall. The king turned pale, his knees shook, and in a faint voice he called for a wise man to tell him what the words meant. But no one could do so. Then the queen spoke. "Let Daniel be called: he will know what this means."

Daniel looked carefully at the writing on the wall: MENE, MENE, TEKEL, UPHARSIN. He said, "MENE means 'number': the days of your reign are numbered. TEKEL means 'weight': you have been weighed in the moral balance and found wanting. UPHARSIN means 'division': your kingdom will be divided between the Medes and the Persians."

That very night Belshazzar was put to death, and Darius, king of the Medes, took possession of the kingdom of Babylon.

IN THE SAME HOUR CAME
FORTH FINGERS OF A MAN'S
HAND, AND WROTE OVER
AGAINST THE CANDLESTICK
UPON THE PLAISTER OF THE
WALL OF THE KING'S PALACE:
AND THE KING SAW THE PART
OF THE HAND THAT WROTE.
DANIEL 5:5

Daniel in the Lions' Den

MEDES
The Medes were closely related to the Persians, and joined forces with them in conquering Babylon. The gold plaque above dates from around 400-300 BC. It shows a Mede, possibly a priest, dressed in a tunic and trousers and wearing a soft, pointed cap.

DARIUS THE MEDE WAS SO IMPRESSED by the wisdom of Daniel that he appointed him the most powerful man in the kingdom, after himself. This made the other officials jealous, and they plotted to bring about Daniel's downfall. But try as they might, they could find no fault in him. "The only way we can harm him," they said to each other, "is to try and make him do something against the laws of his God."

At their request, Darius issued a ruling that for the next thirty days no one should pray to any god, but only to the king himself. Any man found disobeying the new law would be thrown to the lions.

Daniel heard of this, but continued to pray to God three times a day before his open window, which looked toward Jerusalem and was in full view of the street. His enemies gathered outside to watch, then went off triumphantly to report him to the king.

Darius was dismayed that his favorite, Daniel, should have been made a victim of his law, but there was nothing he could do to save him. With a heavy heart, he gave the order for Daniel to be thrown into the lions' den. "Your God will save you," he said to Daniel, and turned away to hide his sorrow. The entrance was then sealed with a heavy stone. That evening Darius refused both food and drink, and lay all night unable to sleep.

Early the next morning the king hurried to where the lions were penned. "Daniel, Daniel," he called. "Has your God protected you?"

"The Lord sent his angel to stand beside me, and the lions have left me untouched."

Darius was overjoyed, and at once gave the order for Daniel's release. Daniel was lifted out of the lions' den unharmed and unafraid, for he knew that God was with him.

Then Darius had all the conspirators arrested, with their wives, and commanded them to be thrown to the lions. At once the beasts fell on them, savagely tearing them apart until there was nothing left of them but bones.

Daniel disobeys the new law by continuing to pray to God

King Darius

MAN-EATING LION
This Phoenician ivory shows a lioness gripping a man by the neck. In the ancient Middle East, people were sometimes executed by being thrown to the lions.

King Darius goes to the lions' den and is overjoyed to find that Daniel is unharmed

The Rebuilding of Jerusalem

King Artaxerxes notices that his cupbearer, Nehemiah, looks unhappy

SILVER CUP
As cupbearer, Nehemiah may have served wine in a silver, horn-shaped cup, such as this one, tasting the wine first to check for poison. A cupbearer held a position of trust, and Nehemiah would have been an influential friend of the king.

SOMETIME EARLIER, Cyrus, king of Persia, had proclaimed that any captive Judeans who wished to return to Judah should be given their freedom. The king had also sent back the silver and gold treasure that had been plundered from the temple by the Babylonians.

The Jewish people who had returned to Jerusalem were saddened to see the state that the city had fallen into – the walls in many places reduced to rubble, the gates blackened by fire. Several of them went to see Nehemiah, cupbearer to Artaxerxes, who was now the king of Persia, to tell him of their damaged city. Nehemiah was so grieved at what he heard that he was unable to hide it from the king while serving wine that evening.

"Why do you look so unhappy?" Artaxerxes inquired. "Are you ill?"

"No, sire," said Nehemiah, "I am not ill, but my heart is breaking because I have been told that Jerusalem, the city of my ancestors, lies in ruins. I beg you to let me go there so that I may start the work of rebuilding." To this Artaxerxes gave his consent, sending with Nehemiah an escort of armed men and letters to the local governors asking them to give him any help he needed.

After Nehemiah had been in Jerusalem for three days, he rode on a donkey by night around the city to see for himself what needed to be repaired. Accompanied by only a few men, he inspected tumbled-down walls and gates that had been half destroyed by fire. Then he summoned the people. "Come, let us rebuild Jerusalem! The condition of our once-great city is a disgrace! Let us pray to God to help us in our work."

Nehemiah gathered together all the volunteers and organized parties of laborers, and gave them directions. But there were some who jeered at his efforts, and threatened to put a stop to the work.

"What do these Israelites think they are doing? Do they really believe that their feeble efforts will make walls out of rubble?"

Some of the men were discouraged, but Nehemiah reassured them.

"Do not be afraid," Nehemiah told his men, "for the Lord is with us, and will protect us." Then he gave spears and shields to half his workforce, and they protected the other half while the repairs were made. And in fifty-two days the work was done.

Nehemiah rides on a donkey by night and inspects the ruined walls of Jerusalem

STONEMASON
Nehemiah would have employed skilled stonemasons to help rebuild Jerusalem. The mason hammered wooden pegs into holes in the rock, then poured water over the pegs. The wood then swelled, causing the stone to split. The mason sawed and trimmed the block with a pick. Stonemasons still practice in parts of the Middle East today.

Index

Who's Who in the Bible Stories

Acknowledgments

Photographic Credits
l=left, r=right, t=top, c=center, b=bottom

ASAP:/Aliza Auerbach 53tr.
A-Z Botanical Collection: 34tl.
BBC Radio Vision: 6br, 7tl.
Bijbels Museum, Armsterdam, 1992: 22tl.
Bridgeman Art Library: 6tl.
Trustees of the British Museum: 17tr, 35br, 58tl, 59br.
Sonia Halliday: 9br, 11tr, 13tr, 16bl, 21tl

27tr, 33tr, 41tr, 45tr, 49tr, 50tl.
Robert Harding Picture Library: 42bl, 46tl.
Hutchinson Picture Library: 7b, 37br.
Image Bank: 30t /J.L. Stage 22bl.
Israel Museum, Jerusalem: 7tr The Shrine of the Book.
Erich Lessing Archive: 15cr, 44bl, 60bl.
Life File: 43tr.
Oriental Institute, Chicago:/John Hudson 51br.
Planet Earth:/Richard Coomber 39br.
Dino Politis: 61tr.
Zev Radovan: 29br.
Spectrum Colour Library: 20bl.
Zefa: 30bl.

DK would like to thank:
Tim Ridley, Nick Goodall and Gary Ombler at the DK Studio; Dorian Spencer Davies; Antonio Forcione; Christopher Gillingwater; Polly Goodman; George Hart; Alan Hills; James W. Hunter; Robin Hunter; Marcus James; Anna Kunst; Michelle de Larrabeiti; Antonio Montoro; Anderley Moore; Jackie Ogburn; Derek Peach; Lenore Person; Dino Politis; Lara Tankel Holtz and Martin Wilson for their help in producing this book.

Picture research by: Diana Morris
Index by: Lynn Bresler